# What Our Readers Have Said...

## Applicability

*"These books are great tools that should be used as guidelines for our everyday supervisory practices. You need to take the time to do a short self-evaluation when reading them."*

•

*"The Pinpoint Training Series delivers information that could be used in a lot different areas."*

•

*"The things and problems we deal with everyday are discussed in these books."*

## Convenience

*"I like this because I can take them with me to read at a convenient time. I feel the little time I have to spend in the office is best use on activities that directly relate to revenue opportunities. I like the short amount of time it takes to keep up with these."*

•

*"I prefer the self-study approach; it fits in with my schedule."*

•

*"I like the fact that the format allows the books to be reviewed as time permits. All work has been conducted on personal, evening/weekend time."*

•

*"Easy to use... if you put the time into it."*

## Challenge

*"My thought is that the real value of these books comes into effect when doing the action plans."*

•

*"I like the fact that the format allows assignments to be reviewed as time permits."*

## Clarity

*"Short and sweet. These books are easy to comprehend."*

•

*"Easy to use, understand, and reference if needed."*

## Relevance

*"I have enjoyed reading these books. They are relevant to today's work environment and the ongoing change in the way we manage our workforce."*

•

*"I believe the contents of the Pinpoint series are excellent. It causes one to reflect on the daily dynamics in working with oneself as well as with management and peers."*

# Becoming a Leader of Your Own Making

*Pinpoint Leadership Skill Development Training Series*

TIMOTHY F. BEDNARZ

MAJORIUM
BUSINESS PRESS

Pinpoint Leadership Skill Development Training Series
*"Becoming a Leader of Your Own Making"*
Timothy F. Bednarz

Graphic design: Monika Pawlak

Majorium Business Press
2025 Main Street
Stevens Point, WI 54481
715.342.1018 • 800.654.4935



ISBN 978-1-882181-69-8

Printed in the United States of America

# Introduction

*The Pinpoint Leadership Skill Development Training Series* is designed for targeted training and education regarding increased improvement in a specific skill or competency.

Each book within this series is designed to be easy to use, understand and apply to your job. It can be used as a basis for training individuals, as a discussion guide or as a personal training tool.

Each chapter within this book discusses a specific concept. When you have completed all eight chapters you should have a 360° perspective of the topic.

Additionally, each chapter is divided into specific sections:

- The first section provides you with an overview of the topic
- The Implications section discusses why the concept is important, and why it is important to learn and apply.
- The Strategies, Tips & Techniques to Apply section teaches how to use and apply the particular concept to your work.
- The Points to Ponder section gives you something to think about or to be discussed with a group setting. These are questions not meant to be immediately answered, but to be pondered over time.
- The Training Activity section provides you with the tools to transfer what you have learned to your job. It is designed to help create an action plan to effectively apply the concept.

Each of the topics in this series is time-tested and proven in the marketplace. They have been used by thousands of employees as training tools. Many of the users have commented that what made these books valuable, was the ability to refer to them when a problem surfaced. They indicated that they remembered reading about the exact problem. They referred back to these books and found an appropriate solution.

You will find them equally valuable as a resource in your professional development library.

# Table of Contents

## LEARNING OBJECTIVES:

- To understand the factors of professional development.
- To identify the benefits of professional development and the impact they have in the professional leadership growth process.
- To apply effective strategies to enhance individual professional development.
- To understand cause and effect relationships and their impact as a result of failing to grow professionally.
- To identify the expected results and outcomes of professional leadership development.
- To apply strategies that effectively enhance professional leadership growth.

# 1

# The Roadmap to Effective Leadership

Leadership effectiveness can be thought of as "an influencing relationship process among leaders and employee followers who work collaboratively to effect real and necessary changes." These changes tend to reflect shared purposes, goals and efforts. It is a dynamic action process focused on mutual understandings and beliefs between leaders and employees.

As there are specific rules and principles that tend to guide leadership vision and actions for effectiveness, leaders need to consider certain questions that ultimately forge their roadmap for success.

The journey toward leadership effectiveness should always begin with a question such as: "What improvement is needed within the organization, and what specific steps do I need to bring it about?" Though senior management typically passes down mandates, timelines and expected goals, it is the individual leader's responsibility to put them into a time lined and vision-directed framework in order to generate positive results.

The roadmap for effective leadership also includes developing higher levels of self-direction, vision, planning and goal achievement, which comes from inspiring others and building cohesiveness, as well as maintaining personal accountability.

In order to begin the path for leadership effectiveness it is important to ask another question: "What's possible here, and how does the organization and its members stand to benefit?"

## IMPLICATIONS — WHAT THIS MEANS TO YOU

A leader's roadmap to effectiveness consists of a series of factors that motivate people to follow. There are four basic qualities that help develop a focus on individual efforts that consistently will lead all involved workplace members beyond routine thinking and performance.

Leader effectiveness is not simply defined by actions made in response to obvious or crisis situations and circumstances. In reality, true effectiveness centers around the ability to move from a "mission impossible" to a "mission outcome" stance. To move consistently forward, leaders need to rely on specific procedures and actions encompassing multiple areas of skill and direction.

## STRATEGIES, TIPS & TECHNIQUES TO APPLY

Elements of management and leader effectiveness often tend to overlap. However, leadership effectiveness is defined in a completely different context. Instead of focusing on basic management principles, practices and procedures as a roadmap for success, the four elements that leaders focus on are self-direction, goal achievement, flexibility and inspiring others to attain greatness. As an integral part of focusing on these factors, leaders recognize the importance of:

### Gaining the Cooperation of Others

Establishing and cultivating a cooperative spirit is one of the primary means of increasing leadership effectiveness. Leaders use it to generate and maintain personal and employee enthusiasm for task and project facilitation. This spirit drives an organization and its people to higher levels of productivity and accomplishment.

Building and establishing a cooperative spirit takes concerted effort and begins with understanding basic human needs and desires. Effective leaders use needs and personal desires to nudge employees in the right direction, while constantly detailing and emphasizing just how motivation works to everyone's benefit.

Making emotional connections is part of the process. This implies being able to evaluate performance and results by measuring them against one's own expectations and goals. It also means acknowledging that as a leader, one needs followers. A truly effective leader builds a sense of workplace interdependence, which is able to gain and produce more in the long term than all combined individual efforts.

The basis for establishing a cooperative spirit lies in examining and analyzing how best to initiate and excel in tasks. Leaders need to be continually identifying their weakest areas, and, in order to improve upon them, need to set specific goals to turn them into strengths. Excelling in tasks and in implementing procedures and assignments helps leaders feel more in control over work-related situations and occurrences, which tends to increase their personal job enthusiasm and stamina.

## Leaders Gain Cooperation by Understanding Their Employees

Beyond workers with a job, effective leaders know their success is inextricably tied to their employees—who like them have concerns, hopes and aspirations. As such, they take the time to converse with and ask questions of their employees. They find out what motivates as well as hinders, frustrates or concerns them. This brings information, concerns, ideas and perspectives to the forefront in order to identify problems, opportunities, and the best actions to take in regard to them.

## Effective Leadership Is Predicated upon the Ability to Listen and Learn

Continuous learning and listening needs to become a top priority if leaders are to excel. Effective leaders never forget where they have been, and use their own as well as others' experiences to dictate where they should go, and why. Learning from past errors in judgment prevents similar types of problems and negative consequences from occurring.

It is essential for leaders to have their ears and eyes on every person, process and situation, not in a controlling sense, but in order to listen for ideas, impending concerns, problems, successes and unhappiness. Effective leaders absorb everything and act on the knowledge they gain to prevent conflict or work slowdowns from occurring. They are watchful for opportunities to make people feel successful, competent and comfortable in the work environment.

Effective leaders further recognize they are not reactive, but proactive by nature, where good listening and learning habits set both a positive example in the workplace and the foundation for corrective action before problems can take root and sap productivity.

## Effective Leaders Sacrifice Self to the Needs of Others

Acknowledging and taking the stance of self-sacrifice is what separates leaders from the rest of the pack. Good leaders set their egos aside. They are not afraid to get involved and help out in various projects or situations alongside the people under their direction. They are flexible, continually slowing down or speeding up as they assess their employee's productivity and individual efforts.

Skilled leaders never set or rescind a rule that becomes disruptive to workplace harmony or to any individual employee. Placing employees' needs first means keeping tasks clear, simple and obvious, which makes for a committed workforce. It means making sure employees know exactly what is expected of them and how to complete the tasks assigned. They also focus on ways to make their own assignments and projects simpler, more direct and clearly defined.

## Success Springs from a Consistent and Positive Workplace Example

Accepting others as they are and embracing differences and unique qualities tends to generate mutual respect and open communication. Thus leaders work at building cohesiveness through cooperative efforts and hold employees and themselves accountable to achieving their goals and vision.

Positive examples can only be set when outward actions correspond with words and do not send a mixed message. Success is entirely dependent upon following through with promises and commitments without deviating from what was promised, even under stress and adversity. Therefore leaders remain inwardly and outwardly genuine, and use discretion in everything they plan, say and do.

## POINTS TO PONDER — SOMETHING TO THINK ABOUT

1. Which one of the preceding factors do you feel is the hardest area in which to remain focused? Why?
2. Do you find it hard to develop consistency in word and action? What factors do you feel have a definite impact upon it?

## TRAINING ACTIVITY — APPLICATION & ACTION PLAN

1. On a piece of paper, create five columns and head them with "Gaining the cooperation of others", "Listening and learning well", "Putting others' needs above my own", "Performing consistently" and "Suggestions."
2. Create two columns next to each, one for "positive actions" and the other for "suggestions to increase efforts."
3. Under each column write down what you are doing daily to achieve each goal.
4. Under the suggestions column, write down one creative idea to increase your effectiveness in each area.

# 2

# Critical Skills that Determine Positive Self-Development

The complexion of business and the workplace are continually changing. The skills required of leaders in the past have become outdated and outmoded by the volatile business environment. Today's leaders are required to change and adapt or lose their professional edge. There are a number of critical skills that need to be mastered in order for leaders to remain a relevant and viable resource for their company.

Most leaders would like to maintain the status quo. It is easy to be resistant to change. In fact, many are doing just that, hoping that conditions will revert to the way they were in the past. Unfortunately, this wishful and myopic thinking produces numerous adverse consequences.

## IMPLICATIONS — WHAT THIS MEANS TO YOU

The dynamic impact of change is a reality that each leader must fully comprehend and come to terms with. This demands that thinking and attitudes continually evolve with increasing ongoing transformations in the global marketplace. New skills are required for leaders to integrate these changes into their business environment and adapt to new ones not far behind.

## STRATEGIES, TIPS & TECHNIQUES TO APPLY

A number of skills must be developed in order to enhance personal and professional development. None of these skills are independent of a leader's job performance, but are in fact strongly linked to it. These include the ability to:

### Think 'Outside the Box'

Most leaders' personal thinking is shaped by the events and circumstances they have previously experienced. Over time, thinking patterns tend to become solely focused on the activities of the company and upon issues and situations related to the effectiveness of their employees. Because of this, reasoning and perceptions often become clouded and stagnant. Many times they include a bias and perspective that does not reflect reality.

Change and its forces really do demand that leaders get outside of their normal way of viewing things to develop a fresh perspective of both their company and the reality of the existing business environment. This often results in a thinking paradigm shift that positively impacts future business practices and methods. It compels leaders to recognize the changing reality of their own business climate, its needs and concerns, and how emerging forces are producing a positive or negative impact on how the business functions. It also works to develop a fresh focus on what is needed to compete effectively, grow and gain market share.

### Change the Culture

Linked with this thinking paradigm shift is a need for effecting a change in the corporate culture. This is necessitated by the various factors brought about by a continuously evolving marketplace. Leaders often have difficulty dealing with the concept of changing the culture around them. This stems mostly from fear of the personal consequences that accompanies corporate transformation and because most of the changes tend to challenge conventional wisdom.

Most leaders don't understand exactly what is required to evolve as truly effective leaders or how to go about it. New methods and ideas conflict with their current managerial roles. They feel at risk because their comfort zones are threatened and new skills in leadership are often lacking. Many worry they will not be able to fill their newer role adequately enough to produce the results the culture change demands.

## Monitoring the Pulse of the Business

A leader's professional development demands that they delegate more daily activities and responsibilities to selected employees. While this pushes decision making down to the front lines—where it has the most impact—it does not mean that leaders should not be continually aware of what is happening in regard to each delegated employee. Rather, they should use some form of metrics system to keep a daily pulse on what is occurring in the workplace. Though they need to delegate their micromanagement activities, there still is the essential need to maintain an active and open presence with their employees or work teams. This allows them to individually and proactively interact whenever required.

## Act Quickly

As leaders formulate their particular leadership style, they must incorporate the ability to act quickly and decisively. In a business environment of rapid change, hesitancy is a liability, especially in the current workplace environment where failure to act can easily create an opportunity for the competition to gain a foothold.

## Keep It Simple

While many leaders are prone to the misconception that the more sophisticated and complicated the plan, the better it is, a good leader understands the need to keep things simple and to stress execution.

Though outwardly impressive, complicated plans and solutions demand complex and costly systems to support them, are prone to human error, and increase the risk of failure. Straightforward and simple plans and goals are less expensive, less subject to human error and far easier to execute.

## Develop Self-Confidence

Leaders who desire to develop their professional skills must cultivate an innate sense of confidence in their decisions. Many stumble into the pitfall of always second-guessing themselves. This results in hesitancy and a loss of self-confidence in their professional abilities. It is a far more desirable leadership trait to act quickly and decisively, then modify the decision as additional data and results become available, than it is to wait until extenuating circumstances develop due to indecision. Inaction only gives rise to additional problems that will also need to be addressed and surmounted.

### POINTS TO PONDER — SOMETHING TO THINK ABOUT

1. How proactive are you in your leadership skills?
2. What prevents you from personally developing each of these required skills?

### TRAINING ACTIVITY — APPLICATION & ACTION PLAN

1. List the following skills on a sheet of paper and identify the specific areas in which you are personally proficient.
    - Thinking 'Outside the Box'
    - Changing the Culture
    - Monitoring the Pulse of the Business
    - Acting Quickly
    - Keeping it Simple
    - Developing Self-Confidence
2. Identify areas of weakness for improvement and based upon your self-assessment, create a program to strengthen each skill set listed above.

# 3

# Becoming a Leader of Your Own Making

Whether the economy returns to robust conditions or continues to perform poorly, one fact remains: market conditions will continue to be unstable. Whole industries grow at dynamic rates, while others collapse with similar rapidity. Yet times of volatility and uncertainty provide the greatest amount of opportunities for leaders willing to take the necessary risks to define themselves.

There was a time when an organization's leaders, and for that matter most corporate managers, had a well-defined life. Their roles were well-established and responsibilities were clearly delineated. Those times have ended, replaced by an era of change and upheaval. The tranquility of yesterday's managerial roles and atmosphere has been displaced by the stress and turmoil of today's new expectations and chaotic environment.

## IMPLICATIONS — WHAT THIS MEANS TO YOU

This is important for leaders to understand because the "direct and control" roles they once had are quickly fading and being replaced by the dynamics of leadership. This process includes embracing and enhancing the elements of empowerment, trust and performance. Leaders, not managers, are the ones to effectively harness the dynamics of change. It is no longer enough to merely direct and control. Evolving conditions demand that leaders emerge with a personal vision of what change itself can accomplish, then enthusiastically communicate their message and its possibilities. Those incapable of transforming themselves into today's effective leaders will be quickly swept away and replaced by others who can.

## STRATEGIES, TIPS & TECHNIQUES TO APPLY

The role of professional development takes on added significance in highly dynamic times such as these. In the past, professional development meant that leaders were adding, enhancing and polishing existing skills for future growth opportunities. Today, professional development requires leaders to transform themselves into becoming dynamic powerhouses that induce and create change all around them.

This process requires newer and more effective leadership styles and roles.

### Leading

Leaders lead while managers direct. Today's leaders must assume a role that allows them to create a personal vision for the future and communicate it with passion and conviction.

It also demands that they become proactive in both their thinking and actions, facing and tackling challenges head on and searching for new opportunities and ways of doing things. This contrasts with the traditional manager's role of reacting to events as they occur, and depending upon the circumstance, taking advantage of only the more obvious opportunities. Today's leaders don't have this luxury. They must search out and find opportunities and take advantage of each one before the competition gains a foothold.

### Learning

Leaders must develop a zeal for learning while they simultaneously create a passionate learning philosophy and climate within their organization. The dynamics of change create the demand for more knowledge and expertise in order to adapt. Traditional training is no longer effective or efficient. Leaders must be in a continuous learning mode, constantly looking for new ideas, insights and concepts that they can translate and apply to their environment and arising situations and events.

## Keeping a Finger on the Pulse of the Business

The principles of leadership include delegation, trust and communication. The applications of these principles require that daily activities, tasks and decisions once held by higher level and general workplace managers, become extensively driven down into lower levels of the organization, directly to the employees in the front lines. Even though by doing this many of the time-consuming tasks are removed, leaders still actively and consistently maintain a finger on the pulse of the workplace and organization as a whole. Deviations from predetermined measurement standards create red flags that are used to identify when their intervention is needed and warranted.

## Continually Taking the Long-Term View

Leaders are more strategic in their thinking and less tactical. They learn to delegate or eliminate time-wasting tasks so that they are more readily available to accomplish their mission. With these tactical responsibilities removed, they are able to develop and hone their strategic thinking capabilities. Strategic thinking is what allows leaders to move their organization forward. More time is available for thinking "outside the box" and to search out new and innovative ways to increase performance and overall results.

## Taking Risks

Active leadership demands that leaders take the necessary risks to move their organization forward. It should be noted that they do not take foolhardy chances or any type of risk without fully considering all potential consequences and ramifications upon everyone involved and the organization itself. Once a situation is assessed and challenged, leaders act quickly and without hesitation. Specific actions are based upon their personal assessments and convictions.

## Keeping an Eye on the Numbers

Effective leaders maintain a close eye on their financial statements, actively monitoring them for wasteful or excessive spending. They develop realistic budgets and strictly adhere to them throughout the year, making modifications when required. When possible they link their sales metrics directly to their budgets. Doing this provides them with a more accurate picture of what is happening daily within their individual work units and organization.

### POINTS TO PONDER — SOMETHING TO THINK ABOUT

1. Do you describe yourself as a dynamic leader, a laid-back manager or somewhere in between?
2. Do you see more of a need to be an effective leader than a successful manager within the current business environment and your organization?

### TRAINING ACTIVITY — APPLICATION & ACTION PLAN

1. Determine how well you are progressing in professional development.
2. Using the list of items below, assess your performance development in each of the given areas.
3. Develop a personal plan to eliminate any deficiencies that may exist.
    - Leading
    - Learning
    - Keeping a Finger on the Pulse of the Business
    - Continually Taking the Long-Term View
    - Taking Risks
    - Keeping an Eye on the Numbers

# 4

# Overcoming Professional Development Hurdles

It's one thing for a leader to know what is needed in order to develop professionally and adapt to changes—and another to do it. Yet while time and other job pressures make any development difficult, it is possible when approached in the proper light.

Whether leaders are formally trained or undertake professional development on their own, the process has a single purpose: to change personal behavior in a way that yields positive results. While some behavioral changes can be spontaneous, most will happen incrementally over time.

## IMPLICATIONS – WHAT THIS MEANS TO YOU

Many leaders feel compelled to change their behaviors quickly, overnight. Attempting to make dramatic and instantaneous changes generally results in additional stress and pressure in an already demanding job.

Good people in leadership roles who are able to noticeably change their behavior understand that change is incremental. Effective leaders understand that by applying what they have learned in smaller steps, they can progress over time to achieve the desired results without creating internal turmoil and pressure.

## STRATEGIES, TIPS & TECHNIQUES TO APPLY

The psychological makeup of many leaders is competitive. Various "type A" personalities compel many to work on a task until they succeed and overcome it, then quickly move on to another. However, this approach to professional development will result in failure and frustration for the following reasons:

### Time

Time is the biggest obstacle to change and professional development. Today's leaders are inundated with so many tasks and responsibilities that any inclination for professional development is quickly pushed aside as more pressing problems and issues demand their energy and time.

This is why an incremental approach to learning and development is markedly more effective. It may take longer—but it will happen, rather than be forgotten or brushed aside. The leader who commits to learning and applying one simple idea or concept a day, or even week, will achieve his or her goals incrementally through continuous persistence. This approach also prevents undue stress and burdens. Incremental change does not overwhelm the leader with an immediate and daunting challenge to learn and adjust.

### Focus

The demands on the average leader result in a loss of personal focus on the long-term professional development goals required to advance their and the company's cause. Leaders must understand the need to focus on these important developmental goals and not sacrifice them for the sake of expediency. Once again, the incremental approach of breaking developmental goals down into small incremental steps allows them to perform their tasks efficiently without sacrificing their professional development.

### Daily Problems

The compelling pressures of daily problems and crises not only continuously divert leaders' attention away from their professional development, but also hinder them in accomplishing their defined goals and objectives. While the demands of the workplace cannot be denied, leaders must devote a small portion of their day or week to accomplishing a small step in their professional development. The key is persistence in both the scheduling and investment of a consistent amount of time.

## Change

The forces and dynamics of change are becoming a more pressing concern for all corporate and business cultures. When the pressures of time, personal focus, daily problems, competition and workplace performance are thrown into the mix, the world can appear spinning out of control. However, it is precisely these factors that make professional development and transformation into as effective a leader as possible essential. Only through adequate development in these skills will a leader be able to make sense of his or her chaotic environment. Rather than push aside the need to develop professional skills, the forces of change should make the average leader embrace the need to learn, adapt and alter behaviors.

## Competition

Intensifying competitive pressures provide today's leaders with yet another barrier to devoting attention to their development. These issues shift their focus to more immediate matters at hand and away from developing their professional skills. Yet the existence of a learning environment where leaders can learn incrementally and apply new ideas, concepts and insights is the answer to dealing with competitive pressures. When leaders afford themselves the opportunity to learn and grow their skills, they are enabling themselves to step "outside the box"—if even for an instant. This can often provide them with insightful solutions to many competitive problems that would otherwise continue to grow or remain unsolved.

## Performance and Motivation

Today's workplace revolves around performance and results. This is the leader's raison d'etre: to ensure all individual members in the organization are performing and producing at all times. This is the biggest challenge facing all leaders, and where the bulk of their time needs to be devoted.

Professional development creates a more efficient and effective leader who then improves overall workplace performance. As a more effective leader, one has the impetus and tools to significantly impact the performance of their individual units and the organization as a whole.

## POINTS TO PONDER — SOMETHING TO THINK ABOUT

1. What are the biggest challenges you face in creating and holding to a successful professional development program?
2. Have you been able to successfully overcome these challenges? If so, how?

## TRAINING ACTIVITY — APPLICATION & ACTION PLAN

Below are listed some of the greatest barriers to change and professional development. Next to each, identify the specific strategies you can use to overcome these obstacles and create a channel for your own professional development.

- Time
- Focus
- Daily Problems
- Change
- Competition
- Performance and Motivation

# 5

# Taking the Right Action Steps

In the face of overwhelming change it is often difficult to predict the future with any certainty. Leaders must have the flexibility to adapt to change and use the methods that best harness its forces to their advantage. In many cases, this results in a paradigm shift in both thinking and actions. While it will be difficult for some leaders to adjust, one thing is certain: today's market, business conditions and organizational workplaces are not friendly to those resistant to change.

Leaders must recognize that many of the traditional management models of the past are just that—obsolete. Many organizations have furthermore used and applied any number of fads over the past decade, to limited or disastrous effect. These new ideas and concepts have often been used with the intent to enrich their authors and creators rather than the company. Yet in volatile times, leaders must deal with the ever-increasing, unrelenting forces of change with a corresponding alteration in their attitudes and by adopting the desire to leave convention behind.

## IMPLICATIONS – WHAT THIS MEANS TO YOU

This is critical for leaders to understand because they are forced to adapt to and align themselves with changes within their industry and company. The traditional role of directing and controlling is being replaced by the principles of active leadership and empowerment simply because both are the most effective tools to use in anticipating, handling and managing change within the organization and workplace. This transforms general management positions into proactive rather than passive roles. In this way a leader is constantly vigilant and prepared to deal with the ever-changing business environment.

## STRATEGIES, TIPS & TECHNIQUES TO APPLY

Leaders must adapt and change to meet the demands of their company, customers and market. Their professional development and transformation into the role of proactive leadership is closely linked to the changes their organization must make to survive and prosper. As change is continuous and pervasive, commitment to the process and evolution of new ideas and professional development must also be ongoing.

### Brainstorming

Leaders must constantly be seeking to implement new ideas and concepts. The best new ideas and insights reside in the native knowledge of their individual employees. Leaders may not be comfortable with this, but the fact is their employees are positioned in the front lines of the business, and as such are far better able to gather direct feedback from both prospects and customers and observe what the competition is doing in the marketplace. Unfortunately in many organizations this wealth of knowledge is seldom tapped, much less converted into a useful form that can be applied to the company's advantage. Yet, various sources of information, insights and ideas are at the leader's fingertips, and they have only to be secure enough in their identity and talent to *use* them.

Today's leaders need to create a mechanism for putting their employees' knowledge into action. The use of brainstorming sessions to develop and work through ideas and concepts is highly suited to this end. Where geographically dispersed workforces prohibit this, leaders should consider a threaded discussion group using email to engage their scattered people as a group.

Brainstorming has distinct advantages in that it feeds on participants' synergy to build on and expand methods, ideas and concepts. Most participants feel energized and motivated when the exercise is properly done, where all ideas and feedback are accorded respect and equal consideration.

## Move Beyond Past Prejudices

Most seasoned leaders have developed personal prejudices about how things in their workplace should be run and done. These stem from their past experiences and successes over the span of their careers. However, these biases can and do actively hinder their ability to develop and implement new ideas and concepts. With the speed and impact of change, what has worked well in the past simply may no longer be effective. The fact that some methods, principles, techniques and concepts are still in place does not mean there are no better ways of doing things. The leader must search out and fully explore them.

New ideas and concepts gleaned during brainstorming or other forms of feedback should not be summarily dismissed as not fitting into the organizational culture. Leaders need to put aside their personal prejudices and examine all viable ideas from various angles and perspectives to determine whether they do have a particular application or function, or if they can work effectively to improve employee and workplace performance.

## Implement New Ideas

While leaders must get new ideas from their employees, counterparts and customers, as well as from their own research, this is not enough. They must develop the ideas gathered and determine each one's applicability in regard to the organization. Leaders must prioritize them and implement the particular ideas likely to create the best impact on results.

While there is always the internal fear that new ideas will not work, leaders must overcome it. The best way to accomplish this is by continually testing new ideas. If the idea does fail, they should learn from the experience and move on to more viable concepts. These failures and learned lessons give rise to new and viable ideas.

## Remove Barriers

Leaders must remove barriers to their employees' effectiveness, productivity and efficiency. In the workplace environment, this typically includes redundant, ineffective or outdated procedures and even superfluous reports that hinder their ability to get work assignments and projects completed efficiently and effectively.

Leaders need to review what is wanted versus what is currently and realistically needed. The implementation of new ideas as well as the increase in customer service levels may require a streamlining of procedures to enhance the workplace's ability to produce and attain desired results.

## Think Small

In the past there was a tendency for companies to expand through acquisitions and mergers with a "bigger is better" mindset. However, today's leaders must think in terms of "smaller is more efficient." This may include a reorganization process that designs and forms smaller and more nimble units. Additionally, thinking small should transfer to the areas of goals and planning. IBM built their business on the philosophy of "small successes generate large dividends." By scaling their goals into a series of easily attainable steps, leaders were able to build their employees' confidence and motivation by reaching one small goal after another. The outcome was the same as giving them an overall goal, but the bar was lowered so as not to seem insurmountable.

## Lead with Passion

As leaders become more proactive, they need to effect a corresponding shift in their styles and energy levels so they are able to lead with passion, sharing and conveying their personal vision with employees, customers and suppliers wherever and whenever practical. They will find this passion contagious, and that it will positively affect and highly impact the overall performance of the entire organization.

## POINTS TO PONDER — SOMETHING TO THINK ABOUT

1. Have you aligned your personal thinking with the changes occurring within your organization, or do you resist new ideas?
2. How passionate are you about effectively leading your employees and implementing new ideas and concepts?

## TRAINING ACTIVITY — APPLICATION & ACTION PLAN

1. Examine the key concepts discussed in this lesson, including:
    - Brainstorming
    - Getting Rid of Past Prejudices
    - Implementing New Ideas
    - Removing Barriers
    - Thinking Small
    - Leading With a Passion
2. Identify the number of ideas you currently are applying on a consistent basis.
3. Determine the depth of their application.
4. Determine any deficiencies in specific applications.
5. Create a plan to implement additional concepts.

# 6

# Maintaining Focus

While it is easy for leaders to start out with the best of intentions, many can be detoured by the uncontrollable events that impact their professional lives and organization. When a crisis occurs leaders often have a tendency to "run toward the sound of the guns" to meet the challenge. While well-intentioned and often necessary, they should not allow this reactive thinking to cause them to lose focus on their goals and professional development.

Maintaining a results-oriented focus takes discipline and perseverance in the face of constant interruptions that demand vast amounts of time and attention. If leaders are totally focused in their thinking, it will be entirely strategic in nature, focused on the long-term growth of the organization, rather than on a reactive solution for an individual problem or crisis, even though it may require their immediate attention. The ultimate solution to every problem needs to fit into the long-term goals the leader has established.

## IMPLICATIONS — WHAT THIS MEANS TO YOU

Maintaining a focus on long-term goals and objectives to attain a desired result is a critical prerequisite for doing the right things, in the right sequence, at the right time. Often leaders allow uncontrollable events and problems to distract them and disrupt their long-term plans, which prevents them from attaining their goals and desired outcomes. Once this happens, many abandon their plans for a later time considered to be more convenient for revisiting and revising them.

## STRATEGIES, TIPS & TECHNIQUES TO APPLY

Leaders desiring to be successful in maintaining a results-oriented focus that allows them to consistently achieve their goals and desired outcomes must:

### Develop Mental Discipline

Successful leaders have developed the mental discipline that keeps them focused on their goals regardless of the problems and uncontrollable events encountered. They view these as hurdles and obstacles to overcome and a normal part of the process on the path to successful attainment of their goals.

Mental discipline allows leaders to continuously keep focused on their goals. These are the mountaintops they constantly keep their eyes on, and, as such, they do not allow daily problems to impede their progress. While some problems may create a setback and cause them to take a detour, they always make sure that they are moving forward—one step at a time. Leaders need to continually remind themselves that developing mental discipline takes a conscious effort, a large dose of patience, and unwavering, ongoing perseverance. While not an easy road, it is certainly achievable.

### Develop Strategic Thinking Skills

To attain and maintain a results-oriented focus, leaders must learn to take the "long view" in regard to their organization. This means acquiring and polishing strategic thinking skills—the skills which allowed them to create their focus in the first place. Strategic thinking needs to become imbedded as a vital component of their personal vision. Together they define the "top of the mountain." A leader's long-term thinking and skill enhancement are part of the active desire to attain it.

This is opposed to tactical thinking skills that focus on short-term, day-to-day activities. As organizations evolve and change, many leaders find it necessary and advantageous to empower more of their employees. They delegate many of these tactical activities to the more skillful and trusted members within individual work units and the organization itself. These delegated employees begin assuming much of the daily decision making that directly impacts their performance and relationships with peers, managerial counterparts and customers.

## Plan

While the concepts of planning were considered passé and outmoded during the booming inception of the dot-coms, it was the lack of adequate planning that ultimately brought about their demise. Successful leaders develop a realistic plan, work the plan and stick to it. This is a simple concept to execute with self-discipline.

It is in the execution of the plan where results are achieved. Many leaders develop good plans and yet fail to reach their goals and desired outcomes because they fall short in effectively executing them. The best plans are not complex instruments, but are designed with an eye toward simplicity and ease of execution.

## Question Activities

Often leaders want to control everything within their personal universe. It is this sense of control that causes many to lose focus as they attempt to personally handle every problem or issue that erupts or surfaces.

Leaders must learn to consistently empower their employees and be open to delegating tasks, assignments and responsibilities that do not actively move them toward their ultimate desired goals and outcomes. In this light, every activity on their to-do list and calendar must be questioned on a consistent basis. If it does not move the leader toward the accomplishment of specific goals, it should be delegated or eliminated for more productive tasks and responsibilities.

## Monitor Results

Successful leaders tie metrics measuring their organization's progress directly to their sales plan. They use them to determine the content and frequency of essential reports. Obtaining various reports and information when needed and in a timely fashion allows them to actively monitor the pulse of their organization and progress toward the attainment of their goals.

Additionally, they have indicators built into their metrics that immediately red flag existing or potential problems when the numbers reported to them fall outside of a predetermined tolerance. This enables them to act quickly and resolve most issues before they spiral out of control.

## POINTS TO PONDER — SOMETHING TO THINK ABOUT

1. Have you developed the mental discipline it takes to maintain a results-oriented focus?
2. Are you easily taken off-focus by daily problems and crises that continuously surface?

## TRAINING ACTIVITY — APPLICATION & ACTION PLAN

1. The following activities and characteristics are not automatically developed and honed into applicable skills. It takes time, patience and discipline.
    - Develop Mental Discipline
    - Develop Strategic Thinking Skills
    - Plan
    - Question Activities
    - Monitor Results
2. Analyze the skill areas above you feel you are proficient in. Determine if there are any deficiencies in your development or applications.
3. Develop a personal plan for each of the above activities or characteristics, including an improvement plan for any skills you feel you already have.
4. Implement your plan and monitor the results.

7

# Creative Decision Making

The events that have transpired over the years since the onset of the early 2000s recessionary cycle, especially beginning September 11, 2001, underscore the turbulent times all organizations face. While uncertainty is troubling, the time of greatest organizational opportunity is found when the business environment is experiencing its greatest turbulence.

If one looks at when the greatest industrial giants started, it was during times of upheaval and turbulence. Greats like Rockefeller, Carnegie and J.P. Morgan emerged out of the shift from an agrarian to an industrial society. Companies like Hewlett-Packard, Apple Computer and Microsoft emerged from the shift to an electronic society. This leap to greatness is made possible by the fact that during times of turbulence many of the traditional paradigms that govern business are shattered. Companies and whole markets begin to seek out new solutions to the problems brought about by the forces of change.

## IMPLICATIONS — WHAT THIS MEANS TO YOU

Creative thinking and decision making can greatly enhance leaders' success during turbulent times. Rather than mourn the loss of business or bemoan internal changes brought about by recessionary pressures or from intensified market competition, leaders begin seeking new opportunities that present themselves in the prevailing market conditions. One thing is certain: organizations are not going back to the business models that governed them in the 90s. They are seeking new ways to enhance productivity and profitability, and therein lies the opportunity for any leader who wishes to seek it out. However, each should acknowledge that in times of turbulence, the ability to anticipate problems, situations and opportunities dramatically increases their chances of success.

## STRATEGIES, TIPS & TECHNIQUES TO APPLY

If leaders wish to take advantage of the turbulence in their markets they must apply creative thinking skills that enhance their decision making and enable them to step 'outside the box.' The resultant shift in thinking allows them to design and develop new solutions to address their workplace and organizational problems. It is also a necessary component for pinpointing available but oftentimes hidden opportunities. These demand a creative thinking process consisting of the following steps:

### Understanding Personal Influences

All leaders are influenced by their own impressions of reality. This creates a personal bias that shapes their perception of the present and future. Typically these perceptions are created from personal and professional past or recurring experiences. This is exemplified by military generals who plan for future wars and conflicts based on lessons learned from past engagements. The leaders that emerged from World War II—Eisenhower, Bradley, Patton—began as colonels and majors. The conflict gave them the ability to shine as leaders.

This highlights the crucial importance of managers transforming themselves into positive and effective leaders. More than ever, today's leaders need to be driven by their zealous view of the possibilities held by the future, as defined by their vision. Leaders learn to rid themselves of their personal biases and look to what is possible and then actively, consistently and passionately work toward specific goals that will achieve it. In this way their perceptions of the past do not negatively influence their outlook on the future: this is where opportunity resides.

Once leaders understand that which impacts and influences their personal perceptions, they can take them into account as they anticipate the future. This allows them to actually step outside of their self-imposed limitations to see things in a creative light as never before—and to think and plan accordingly.

## Divergent Thinking

Leaders must apply divergent thinking skills to understand and discover more than one right answer to any problem. Included in this classification is the "what if" thinking scenario. Divergent thinking allows leaders to seek the possibilities and opportunities that present themselves. Additionally, polished divergent thinking skills allow leaders to remove the personal biases and perceptions that normally work to distort or eliminate creative possibilities. Doing this aids them in fully exploring all possibilities, thoughts and ideas from various perspectives and angles.

## Convergent Thinking

Once leaders have examined all of the possibilities available to them, they must use convergent thinking skills to focus on the integration of data and prioritize available choices. This is where leaders apply analysis skills to determine the economic feasibility of each choice and determine its impact and the ramifications upon the organization and workplace.

## Mapping

Mapping, another word for planning, is the leader's capacity to draw the pathways that show how he or she will get from the present to the future. In others words, it is the ability to formulate objectives that lead the organization toward the accomplishment of the overall goal or desired outcome.

## Imaging

Imaging is the ability to draw visual pictures or representations using words, graphs, models or drawings to effectively communicate the vision and intended course of the organization. This allows a leader to effectively communicate his or her vision of its future direction and to highlight opportunities as they present themselves. It is vital that leaders present options, opportunities, ideas and pathways to the vision's attainment in a way that can be easily understood by their employees and others.

## POINTS TO PONDER — SOMETHING TO THINK ABOUT

1. Do you perceive the current times as a period of opportunity or survival?
2. What hinders you from identifying various opportunities that may be present for your organization?

## TRAINING ACTIVITY — APPLICATION & ACTION PLAN

1. On a sheet of paper list all of the perceptions you have about your organization and its products as well as the industry as a whole and its customers.
2. Next to each perception, identify what has created it in your mind.
3. Determine if each impression is accurate and realistic.
4. Identify those perceptions that may have been the result of faulty thinking or misconceptions about the future.

# 8

# Obtaining the Results You Want from Your Leadership Role

In order to get the best results possible from their leadership efforts, leaders need to prepare for them. Most corporations require leaders to produce an annual plan to project possible future results. Many leaders tend to undertake this assignment with little or no enthusiasm even though it is necessary to forge new paths to generating positive, successful outcomes. Once completed, most annual plans sit on the shelf until the next planning cycle. Many times the rationale is that people are too involved and overwhelmed with daily activities to follow their plan.

Effective leaders tend to view planning as a means to generate, oversee and measure results. Planning gives leaders time to consider how they can improve their own as well as overall workplace performance. It allows leaders to reflect on ways to stretch their employees' abilities in order to make them a more viable resource for generating and enhancing long-term results.

Leaders must recognize that preparing for results does have its challenges, and be aware of them before beginning their next planning cycle.

## IMPLICATIONS – WHAT THIS MEANS TO YOU

During planning and budgetary reviews, leaders sometimes develop unreliable projected numbers and assumptions. It is all too easy to develop projections without specific facts to back them up, yet obtaining positive end results relies on sound forecasting. Many leaders fail to invest the needed effort to review past performance, and this deficiency tends to affect their end outcomes. Some also fall short in taking the necessary time to effectively base future projections and assumptions upon what their organizational units have actually achieved in the past, which distorts expectations.

Obtaining results implies that plans and budgets not be developed in a void. Effective leaders realize that they must build on past successes and determine why and how past failures occurred. They know that to increase results it is essential to plan for strengthening weak and non-performing areas. Leaders can only accomplish this by thoroughly reviewing past performance in all areas in order to link plans to where the organizational unit currently stands. Performance reviews allow leaders to accurately project their organizational unit's performance forward in incremental steps. This is the only realistic method of achieving and sustaining growth.

## STRATEGIES, TIPS & TECHNIQUES TO APPLY

As leaders begin the planning process to increase performance and results, they need to address five specific areas that tend to create the greatest challenges:

### Faulty Assumptions

Every plan that is designed to increase results needs to be based upon a series of assumptions. Consisting of future and anticipated variables that impact the actual performance of the plan, assumptions include economic conditions, sales and production forecasts, as well as anticipated major orders.

If assumptions are inaccurate, plans will be worthless and future results will not be realized. For example, if a plan is based upon 10% growth when in reality the economy is causing a 10% decline, everything in the plan is based upon an inaccurate assumption.

When developing their plans, leaders must focus on carefully creating, listing and detailing accurate and realistic assumptions. As conditions change during the year, reviewing assumptions becomes a necessary procedure in order to adjust them to actual conditions. This enables leaders to quickly alter and adapt their plans throughout the year, ensuring the likelihood of obtaining the results they want.

## Inaccurate Information

To get results, the development and use of accurate information within the planning process is essential. Accurate information is one of the most important aspects of planning and the most significant step in the plan's implementation process. Leaders must take the opportunity to examine every aspect of their organizational unit's past performance. This includes reviewing past plans and budgets against actual performance. Results-oriented leaders understand what worked in the past and why. They identify areas for improvement, revision, modification or an increased workforce. They then focus on underlying causes that tend to influence or precipitate inadequate employee performance. Leaders who make it a point to conduct exhaustive performance reviews are able to produce accurate information and data, which helps to generate higher levels of results over shorter periods of time.

Once leaders produce a comprehensive review, it becomes much easier to update and maintain their information with a higher degree of accuracy. Leaders use the planning process to audit their information and insure its reliability and accuracy.

## Pitfalls to Effective Plan Development

The first major planning pitfall that definitely affects positive end results lies in leaders choosing to create new strategies by simply duplicating previous annual plans with one or two selective changes. Most often changes include simply altering numbers to reflect current conditions. The completed plan is then submitted to senior management. These plans have little value in terms of results-oriented direction or particular action steps to follow.

A second major pitfall is found in writing plans from a "backward perspective." This is where plans are made according to where leaders *want* to go, rather than on where they *should* be going. Strategies are developed without regard to the specific facts, data, timelines and information needed to ensure they are accurate and realistic.

All pertinent information and related data supporting various desired outcomes must be included when generating plans, with all other information that tends to conflict with the desired outcomes omitted.

Both pitfalls are attempts to short-circuit the planning process or avoid it, and greatly reduce the chances of obtaining the results leaders need to generate. When this happens, leaders fail to meet their responsibilities to themselves, employees, associates, senior management and stockholders.

## Impossible Plan Timetables, Allotments and Factors

How plans are scheduled can have a major impact on whether or not results are obtained. Many leaders often assume they can achieve more than is realistically possible to attain. They tend to insert and carry over expectations of impossible timelines and deadlines for employees to follow and meet.

Performance plans should stretch each organizational unit and members' capabilities. Time allotments to move processes and actions along toward achieving goals and objectives must be realistic. Additional time must be factored in for unanticipated events that will inevitably occur during the year. It is essential for leaders not to under-plan, where employees are not pushed to perform. Equally as important they should not over-plan, where employees are constantly placed under stress to meet deadlines. To get better results, leaders must consider the need to balance their plan's time requirements, workload criteria and expectations.

## Failing to View Performance Plans as Positive Management Tools

Often leaders will produce required plans and forget about them until the next ones are due. It is a serious mistake to view planning as an impediment to their work and daily responsibilities.

Results-oriented leaders appreciate how and why performance plans are powerful management tools. Plans guide and direct their actions throughout the year toward the accomplishment of their goals and objectives, which always move them to securing higher levels of workplace results. Results-oriented leaders focus on taking their plans and breaking them down into smaller monthly plans, which can be easily monitored and altered. Leaders also make certain to generate smaller step-by-step plans for every individual employee. This process tends to link both time and individual performance toward the accomplishment of common goals and objectives.

Planning is a continuous, ongoing process. Performance plans need to be continually revisited, modified and adapted to reflect actual conditions. Situations change and performance plans should allow leaders to readily anticipate and adapt to fluctuations, speedups and slowdowns, as well as unforeseen occurrences.

### POINTS TO PONDER — SOMETHING TO THINK ABOUT

1. Did you consider all five challenge areas above when you developed your last planning project?
2. Have you utilized your last completed plan to its fullest to get the results you wanted? Why or why not?

## TRAINING ACTIVITY — APPLICATION & ACTION PLAN

1. Select one or more area(s) of the planning process that you feel needs some improvement. Refer to the challenges mentioned above.
2. Develop strategies and ideas to make the planning process stronger, more reliable and workable.
3. Think of ways to make your planning process more streamlined in terms of time, focus and flexibility.
4. Write these suggestions down before you begin the actual planning process. Refer to them regularly as a reminder.
5. Set up a timeline for your personal planning process. Use realistic timelines for its completion.

# About the Author

Timothy F. Bednarz, Ph.D. is CEO of the American Management Development Group, Inc. For over 20 years he has researched, designed and authored hundreds of learning and development programs used by Fortune 1000 companies.

He is also the author of *Great! What Makes Leaders Great. What They Did, How They Did It and What You Can Learn from It* (2011).

## Speaking Availability

Timothy F. Bednarz, Ph.D. is available for speaking engagements for your next meeting or association event. He can be contacted at 800-654-4935 or by e-mail at timothy.bednarz@majorium.com.

## Bulk Sales

Bulk sales of this book or any other titles available from Majorium Business Press. Inquiries can be directed to sales@majorium.com, or by phone at 800-6654-4935.

# Quick Order Form

**Fax orders:** 715-342-1118. Send this form.

**Telephone orders:** Call 800-654-4935 toll-free. Have your credit card ready.

**Email orders:** sales@majorium.com

**Postal orders:** Majorium Business Press, 2025 Main Street, Stevens Point, WI 54481, USA.

**Please send the following books:**

____________________________________________

____________________________________________

____________________________________________

____________________________________________

**Please send more FREE information on:**

❑Catalog ❑Speaking/Seminars ❑Mailing Lists ❑Consulting

Name: ________________________________________

Address: _______________________________________

City: _____________________ State: ____ Zip: ________

Telephone: ______________________________________

Email address: ____________________________________

**Sales tax:** Please add 5.5% for products shipped to Wisconsin addresses.

**Shipping by air:**

**United States:** $4.00 for first book and $2.00 for each additional product.

**International:** $9.00 for first book; $5.00 for each additional product (estimate).

Made in United States
Cleveland, OH
06 November 2026

47678350R10030